UPLOADING THE FIRE DOWNLOADING THE GRACE

CONTEMPLATIVE PRAYERS

Sharon Jones, LMFT

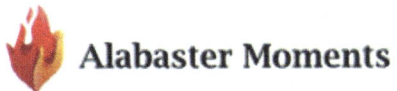

Copyright © [2024] by [Sharon Jones]

All rights reserved.

No portion of this book may be reproduced in any form without written permission from the publisher or author, except as permitted by U.S. copyright law.

DEDICATION

This Book Is Dedicated to My Father, Joe L Franklin (Tunu)

SHARON JONES, LMFT

MY MANTRA

THE TIME YOU SPEND WITH YOURSELF IS THE MOST IMPORTANT TIME IN THE WORLD

OVERVIEW

Uploading the Fire, Downloading the Grace is a transformative and soul-stirring collection of contemplative prayers designed to ignite your inner fire and guide you toward divine grace. Every prayer, sentence, and word is infused with sacred intention, emerging from the deepest, most holy places of the Spirit.

This book serves as a sanctuary for those seeking hope, healing, and spiritual renewal. Thoughtfully constructed and beautifully expressed, it offers profound wisdom and genuine encouragement to all who journey through its pages.

More than just a book, Uploading the Fire, Downloading the Grace is a companion for transformation—a gift of empowerment that helps you rekindle your spirit and embrace grace with open arms. Whether you seek solace, strength, or divine inspiration, these words will illuminate your path, meeting you exactly where you are with truth and goodness.

Let this work become your guide, your source of strength, and your beacon of grace. Begin your journey today, and let the fire within you burn brighter than ever before.

COMTEMPLATIVE PRAYER

Contemplative prayer is a deep, silent form of prayer that emphasizes being fully present with the Creator in quietness, love, and awareness. It focuses on a personal relationship with the divine that transcends words, images, and structured concepts. Rather than making petitions or speaking to the Almighty, it involves simply being in spirit, listening, and opening one's heart.

PURPOSE

Contemplative prayer strengthens one's relationship with the divine, fosters sublime serenity, and nurtures inner transformation, focusing on communion with God rather than making specific requests. It is sometimes described as "resting in God" and allowing God's love and presence to permeate one's entire being.

KEY FEATURES

Silence is a mental and emotional quieting that allows us to hear the divine's silent, small voice.
Stillness is a purposeful pause from action and distractions, focusing exclusively on the Almighty.
Receptivity is the act of letting go of our own ambitions and being open to whatever the Creator reveals.
Union is the desire to connect intimately with the love of God and the divine presence, producing a sense of oneness.

UPLOADING THE FIRE, DOWNLOADING THE GRACE

Contents

ABUNDANCE	1
BEYOND	3
COMPASSION	5
COUNTLESS	8
ENCOURAGE	11
ENDURANCE	13
FAITHFUL	15
FORGIVENESS	17
GRACE	19
GRATITUDE	22
HEALING	24
HEART	26

HOPE	28
INNER PEACE	31
LOYALTY	33
MINDFULNESS	36
PATIENCE	38
PERSONAL GROWTH	41
POWER	43
PRESENCE	46
PURPOSE	49
RENEWAL	52
REPAIR	55
RESILIENCE	58
RESTORATION	61
SATURATE	64
SOURCE	66
SURRENDER	68
THANKSGIVING	70
TRANQUILITY	72
TRUST	74

WISDOM	77
YOUR COMTEMPLATIVE SPACE	80
ACTION STEPS	81
BELIEFS	83
BLESSINGS	84
CARE	85
EVALUATE YOUR SPIRIT	86
HOPE	87
IGNITE THE FIRE	89
THOUGHTS	90
THANK YOU NOTES	91
MEET THE AUTHOR	92

ABUNDANCE

Gracious Spirit,

Showers of blessings come to me in miraculous ways. I notice and appreciate them. So often, in the rush of daily life, I overlook the small yet profound gifts that fill each moment.

I am thankful for the love of family and friends, the beauty of nature, and the gift of breath that sustains me. I recognize the challenges I have faced and am grateful for how they have shaped me, strengthening my faith and building resilience within.

Guide me to cultivate a heart of gratitude so that I may see each new day as an opportunity to appreciate the simple joys and the remarkable moments that often go unnoticed. May my actions and words reflect this thankfulness, sharing the love and kindness that flow from deep within.

As I give thanks, let me also remember those who are struggling. Inspire me to be a beacon of hope and encouragement, offering light where there is darkness.

Thank You for Your constant, unwavering presence in my life. I am truly blessed, and my heart overflows with gratitude for all that has been given and all that is to come.

Please remain with me.

Amen.

BEYOND

Gracious Spirit,

I humbly ask for the strength to look beyond my immediate circumstances and embrace the larger picture. Help me to see the presence of the divine in each moment—whether filled with joy or challenge—and to recognize the beauty in simple, everyday things. Guide me toward a heart of thankfulness, even in times of difficulty.

I lift those who struggle to feel gratitude, even when blessings surround them. May they feel

Your embrace, knowing that they are never truly alone. Help me to share the story of Your unwavering love and faithfulness, so that I may offer encouragement and hope to others.

In my own journey, I bring forth my doubts and struggles, trusting that the divine values my honesty. I release my burdens, choosing to trust in divine timing and the unfolding of life's plan. Help me to let go, to surrender my worries, and to place my trust fully in what is yet to come.

Thank You for the grace that enables growth and transformation. May my thankfulness inspire me to be a source of love and compassion, sharing the abundance I have received with others. Let my life reflect the blessings I have been given and may the fruits of my spirit be a testimony of Your constant care.

I commit to seeking first the divine presence, acknowledging every gift with gratitude and walking the path of faith.

Please remain with me.

Amen.

COMPASSION

Gracious Spirit,

In this moment of submission, I come seeking healing for my body, mind, and spirit. In the vastness of divine power, there is restoration, and I trust in the boundless ability to restore what has been broken and renew what has been lost.

As I face life's struggles and suffering, I ask for comfort and peace to settle within me; to heal the visible and invisible wounds, bringing serenity back to my heart; to let go of the burdens that weigh down my spirit, replacing them with light and love; to be granted the strength to forgive myself and others, opening the door to healing through this act of compassion; to help release bitterness and resentment, making space for understanding and a heart full of empathy; to let forgiveness be the path that leads to renewal.

My mind is clear and pathways of peace quiet my soul. Guide each step toward the paths that lead to joy and wholeness, and surround me with the love of those who uplift me. May I be a source of healing and support for others, sharing the light of restoration I receive.

Gratitude fills my heart for the gift of grace and the promise of renewal. In the journey toward healing, trust remains that all things are possible through the process of rebirth. May compassion and understanding continue to grow within, transforming anger and pain into peace and love.

As I seek restoration, may the clarity of purpose grow stronger with each day. Let me be surrounded by those who bring encouragement and guide me toward becoming a force of healing in the world.

Grateful for the promise of transformation, I place my trust in the flow of divine grace, knowing true healing is within reach.

Please remain close.

Amen.

COUNTLESS

Gracious Spirit,

I feel a heart full of gratitude, acknowledging the countless flow of blessings into my life, both seen and unseen. Each breath is a gift, each day a reminder of the preciousness of life. I give thanks for the love of family and friends, for the beauty found in nature, and for the grace that sustains me in every moment.

Help me to recognize the abundance that surrounds me, especially in times of difficulty.

Teach me to find joy in the simple things — the warmth of sunlight, the laughter of loved ones, the quiet moments of peace and reflection. Let me never overlook the everyday wonders that fill my days.

Gratitude fills my soul for the unwavering presence that brings hope and strength — a comfort that never wavers. Remind me to extend this same love and grace to others, reflecting kindness in my actions, in my words, and in every gesture.

As life unfolds with its complexities, guide me to maintain a spirit of thankfulness even in the face of trials. Let my heart remain anchored in the knowledge that all things are working together for good, though the path may not always be clear. May trust in the divine plan lead me through each day with patience and peace.

May gratitude shape the way I move through the world, influencing every interaction, nurturing relationships, and creating spaces of encouragement. Let my words inspire, reminding others of the blessings they, too, carry.

SHARON JONES, LMFT

For all that has been provided and all that is yet to come, I give thanks. May every action reflect the gratitude within. May I live each day with purpose and intention.

Please remain near.

Amen.

ENCOURAGE

Gracious Spirit,

Favor is providing healing for myself and for those I hold dear. In moments of suffering, I trust in the power to heal both body and soul, knowing that divine compassion and strength are available in times of need.

Grant healing to all those who suffer — whether physically, emotionally, or spiritually. Provide the fortitude to endure hardships and surround them with the peace and love that comes from divine presence. May all feel the comfort that comes from knowing they are never alone, no matter the pain they face.

Bestow upon me the wisdom to care for my own body, mind, and spirit, so that I may also offer love and compassion to others in need. Inspire me to nurture both myself and those around me, and to extend hope to those who feel broken or lost.

Gratitude fills my heart for the gift of faith and the power it brings to heal. I surrender my anxieties and fears, trusting in the flawless plan that will bring healing and wholeness to all.

May divine presence remain steadfast, guiding me through this journey.

Amen.

ENDURANCE

Gracious Spirit,

Aware of my own limitations, I come seeking the strength that lies beyond my own. In times of struggle, I call upon the divine power that can carry me through. When weariness sets in, revive my spirit and remind me that strength is found not within myself but in the sacred presence that sustains me.

Grant me the courage to face each day with bravery and unshakable faith. Help me to navigate my challenges and remain steadfast in the promises of growth and transformation. May strength flow into me so that I can continue, trusting that every trial is shaping me into the person I am meant to be.

I am deeply grateful for the anchor of divine power that supports me, knowing that it is this strength that fuels me forward.

May this presence never depart but remain as a constant source of guidance and renewal.

Amen.

FAITHFUL

Gracious Spirit,

In moments of uncertainty and struggle, I turn to the one constant source of strength and light. When my own strength falters, when the way ahead feels unclear, it is the divine presence that carries me through.

I lay before the Spirit my anxieties, my doubts, and my burdens, seeking the peace that only the divine can provide. Help me to trust more fully, to surrender my fears, and to find comfort in knowing that nothing is hidden from the Creator. Even during imperfection, love remains constant.

Grant patience, compassion, and the ability to recognize purpose in every circumstance. Draw me nearer to this divine presence, help me grow in wisdom and understanding, and remind me that I am never alone.

May the Spirit's love continue to guide and strengthen me, every step of the way.

Amen.

FORGIVENESS

Gracious Spirit,

I have shown up with a heart burdened by resentment and pain. I confess the weight of these feelings I carry and I ask for Your help in releasing them. I know that holding onto this resentment only keeps me from finding peace.

Grant me the courage to let go of the past and help me understand that forgiveness is not just for others but a gift I give to myself. I humbly forgive those who have hurt me, remembering

Your forgiveness of me, releasing the negative hold that anger has over me.

Open my heart to see others through Your eyes — to understand their struggles and offer them compassion instead of judgment. Let Your love open my heart and bring me the healing I need, so that I may forgive and move forward with peace.

Guide me on this journey of healing and strengthen me to accept the grace of forgiveness, both for others and for myself.

Please remain with me.

Amen.

GRACE

Gracious Spirit,

I open myself to Your presence, inviting healing into every part of my body, mind, and spirit.

Let grace flow over my pain and sorrow. Help me release the bitterness, anger, or resentment that weighs down my heart. May any brokenness within be mended, replaced with peace and renewal. Grant me the strength to face my struggles and the understanding to see their purpose in shaping my journey.

I lift all those who suffer — whether from physical illness, emotional pain, or spiritual turmoil. Surround them with comfort and strength, bringing solace where there is despair. Guide those who provide care, filling their hearts with wisdom, compassion, and skill as they work to restore well-being.

Help me to recognize the importance of self-care and to seek the support needed for my own healing. Remind me that I am not alone and that Your presence accompanies me through every step and every challenge. Teach me patience and trust in the process of restoration.

As healing takes place within me, may I become an instrument of healing for others. Empower me to share my journey with honesty and hope, offering encouragement to those navigating their own paths toward wholeness. I am transformed in Your haven.

Thank You for the promise of renewal and the possibility of making all things new. May Your light guide me forward on this path of healing and growth, illuminating each step with peace and purpose.

Remain near always.

Amen.

GRATITUDE

Gracious Spirit,

My heart is full of gratitude for the precious gifts bestowed upon me. Thank You for the beauty that surrounds me each day, for the gift of life itself, and for the love of family and friends. Help me to recognize and cherish even the smallest moments of grace and joy in my life.

Teach me to focus on the lessons You are revealing to me and help me see the hidden blessings, even in times of struggle. May my heart overflow with gratitude, allowing it to shift my perspective and uplift my spirit.

Guide me to be a source of encouragement to others, to lift those around me, and to share my thankfulness in ways that bring light and positivity to their lives. Let my life stand as a testament to Your unwavering presence and goodness.

Thank You for Your constant love and support. I am truly blessed and I am deeply grateful for Your steadfast guidance.

Please remain with me.

Amen.

HEALING

Gracious Spirit,

I notice my heart is heavy with the need for healing — physical, mental, and spiritual. I acknowledge the suffering, the burdens, and the moments that feel too much to carry alone.

I ask for a divine presence to cover me and my loved ones, bring hope to those who are lost in despair, strength to those whose spirits are broken, and rest to the weary. Through Your perfect love, heal both the wounds we see and those hidden deep within, and guide us toward wholeness once more.

Grant me the trust to embrace Your plan, even when the path feels unclear. May I find peace in the knowledge that You walk beside me every step of the way, leading me toward renewal and recovery.

Give me the courage to seek help when I need it and the grace to be a source of support for others on their own journeys of healing. Remind me that healing is not an instant destination but a journey, and that in my struggles, I am never alone.

Thank You for Your unwavering love, compassion, and presence. My trust is in knowing that all things are possible.

Please remain with me.

Amen.

HEART

Gracious Spirit,

I trust in boundless kindness and mercy. Before I even speak, You know the needs of my heart, the burdens I carry, and the struggles within me. I set an intention for healing to flow through me, restoring my body, mind, and soul. Heal the wounds I cannot see and give me the strength to move forward.

In Your presence, help me find peace and serenity. Love replaces every broken or weary part of me. You, who are gentle and compassionate, help me release my pain into Your hands, trusting that You will carry it for me.

I am thankful for unwavering hope, for You being my refuge and my healer. I trust in Your promises, knowing that in Your care I will be restored.

Please remain with me, guiding me every step of the way.

Amen.

HOPE

Gracious Spirit,

My soul is searching for hope. In moments of despair and uncertainty, help me feel Your light shining in my life. I pray for Your divine touch to heal my wounds, both seen and unseen, and to restore me from within.

Help me understand that healing is a journey, not a destination. Grant me the patience to trust Your plan and allow it to unfold in its own time. When I feel discouraged, remind me that each new day is a chance for renewal, a step closer to wholeness. Let Your presence surround me, bringing peace and strength as I move through this process of healing.

I pray for all those in need of physical, emotional, and spiritual recovery. Wrap them in Your love and kindness, guiding them toward healing. May they find comfort in knowing they are not alone in their struggles. Help us all be a source of support for one another, offering compassion to those in need.

Teach me to find joy, even amid hardship. Show me how to see the beauty in the lessons adversity brings and help me hold onto hope as my steady anchor. May I place my trust in Your plan, believing that all things are working together for my good.

As I heal, may I become a light for others, sharing Your love and goodness along the way. Let my journey inspire others to seek Your healing power and find strength in their own paths to recovery.

SHARON JONES, LMFT

Thank You for Your unfailing presence and the promise of restoration.

Please never leave me.

Amen.

INNER PEACE

Gracious Spirit,

I am tuned in and fully aware of my limitations and the weakness of my own strength. In this moment, I seek Your divine power to carry me through the challenges I face. When I feel weary and overwhelmed, remind me that You are my strength and that You have always been by my side, providing what I need.

Grant me the courage to face each day with faith and bravery. Help me to navigate my struggles with perseverance and trust in Your promises. Strengthen my resolve to keep moving forward, knowing that each challenge I encounter is shaping me into the person You have destined me to become.

Thank You, Spirit, for being my pillar of support. I am deeply grateful for Your unwavering presence, which gives me the strength to continue, no matter the obstacles before me.

Please do not leave me.

Amen.

LOYALTY

Gracious Spirit,

I am deeply thankful for everything You have given me — both the tangible and the intangible gifts that fill my life. Your presence is a constant reminder of Your grace, a steady light that guides me through both the calm and challenging times.

I know that You are the source of all beauty and I ask You to inspire me to deeply appreciate the abundance that surrounds me. May I find joy in the love of those around me, in the small pleasures of daily life, and in the splendor of the natural world. Help me see the blessings in every moment, large and small.

As I reflect on my own blessings, help me to see others through the lens of compassion. Fill my heart with love and a desire to share, to give my resources and talents to those in need. Teach me that true abundance is not found in what I possess but in how I serve and uplift others.

Guide me toward a life of abundance, one that is focused on opportunities rather than limitations. Help me embrace a mindset of faith, trusting that You provide all I need and that You are always working in my life for my good.

When doubt creeps in, remind me of Your faithfulness. Help me trust in Your promises, knowing that You are loyal to Your Word and that You will meet my every need. Let my trust in Your provision be a testimony to others, encouraging them to seek You and experience the depth of Your love.

Thank You for the gift of today. As I reflect on this day, I come with an open heart, ready to receive the benefits You have planned for me. In all that I do, may I reflect Your light, becoming a source of hope and encouragement to those around me.

Please do not leave me.

Amen.

MINDFULNESS

Gracious Spirit,

I come with a heart of focus. I recognize the countless blessings, both big and small, that You have graciously given me throughout my life. During the busyness and chaos of each day, help me to pause and acknowledge Your steady hand guiding me, supporting me, and leading me through every moment.

Remind me to stay present in the now, to truly experience the beauty that surrounds me—the warmth of a smile, the love of family and friends, the vibrancy of nature. May I cultivate an attitude of thankfulness that reflects Your boundless kindness, taking joy in the simple gifts that each moment holds.

Grant me the ability to release my anxieties and distractions, allowing me to focus on the here and now. Teach me how to breathe deeply and rest in Your presence, feeling peace in Your company. Even in moments of chaos, help me find gratitude, knowing that there are lessons and blessings hidden in the challenges.

Open my heart to the opportunities around me to serve others and to show appreciation through kind acts and thoughtful gestures. Let my life reflect Your love, encouraging others to walk in joy and gratitude as they journey through their own lives. Thank You for the gift of today.

Please do not leave me.

Amen.

PATIENCE

Gracious Spirit,

I claim a positive outcome that my body, mind, and soul are healed and restored. I believe in Your ability to repair what is damaged and revitalize what is worn out because You are the Great Physician. When I am hurting or distressed, I go to You for support and consolation.

Please use Your healing hands to touch me. I bring all my troubles to You, whether spiritual, emotional, or physical, knowing that You know my innermost wants and pains. Please help me to let go of my troubles so that Your serenity can flow over me like a soft stream.

Give me patience and endurance as I embark on my healing journey. Please remember that restoration is a procedure and I discover a chance to become closer to You at every step. Allow me to accept the lessons I have learned from suffering and turn them into evidence of Your faithfulness.

Please help me to be receptive to other people's assistance during this period. Put me in the company of kind and supportive people who will support me on my path to recovery. May we share the light of Your love and encourage one another.

Please give me the capacity to show kindness and compassion to everyone while I am healing. May I serve as a conduit for Your love, providing solace to those in need. Allow others who need Your healing power to find hope in my recovery.

We are grateful for Your unfailing kindness and the promise of renewal.

SHARON JONES, LMFT

Please do not leave me.

Amen.

PERSONAL GROWTH

Gracious Spirit

I am finally ready to embrace the growth and change You have prepared for me. I accept the path set before me, trusting in Your wisdom and grace to guide my steps. Thank You for the gift of each new day — a blank canvas on which to paint learning, transformation, and renewal.

I humbly ask for Your guidance as I seek to expand my understanding, deepen my insight, and cultivate compassion within my soul. Shine

Your light on the areas of my life that need attention and reveal the changes I must embrace to walk in alignment with Your purpose. Grant me the courage to face my fears, the humility to learn from my missteps, and the perseverance to move forward with faith and intention.

Help me to be patient and gentle with myself on this journey of self-discovery. Teach me to celebrate even the smallest steps forward, finding joy and gratitude in the process of becoming who You have called me to be. Surround me with souls who inspire and uplift me — those who encourage me to step beyond my comfort zone and pursue my highest potential with hope and determination.

I am deeply grateful for Your boundless love and unshakable faith in me. With Your strength, I embrace the process of growth and transformation, confident that I do not walk this path alone.

Please remain with me, steadying my heart and guiding my every step as I move forward in trust and purpose.

Amen.

POWER

Gracious Spirit,

In the silence, my heart is longing for healing and restoration. The weight of anguish and struggles press heavily on my spirit, and in this moment of vulnerability, I turn to You: the ultimate source of comfort and renewal.

Touch my life with Your healing power. Restore me, both in the wounds that are seen and those hidden deep within. Bring wholeness to my body, mind, and soul. I hold fast to the promise that by Your stripes, healing is mine. Help me release the grief, bitterness, and pain I cling to, and teach me the freedom of forgiveness. May I extend the same grace to others that You have so freely given to me.

Remind me that restoration is not only possible but promised, even amidst my struggles. Strengthen my belief in the beauty of Your transformative power. I also lift those who need healing, whether from illness, trauma, sorrow, or loss. Let my spirit feel the presence and assurance of never being alone. Pour out Your healing over them and breathe renewal into their lives.

Thank You for Your unchanging love and kindness. Even when I cannot see the path ahead, I trust that You are working in my life. I surrender my fears and anxieties, placing my future in Your capable hands.

Let the bonds we share with You bring us peace and joy as we walk forward in faith. May Your Spirit flow through every part of our being, restoring us completely and drawing us closer to Your purpose for our lives.

Thank You, Gracious Spirit, for being my refuge and my healer.

Please remain with me always.

Amen.

PRESENCE

Gracious Spirit,

I am deeply aware of the blessings that fill my life. Thank You for the abundance I experience — the love of friends and family, the beauty of the natural world, and the small joys that make each day a precious gift.

I am grateful for moments of happiness and peace that remind me of Your presence and Your sustaining care. Help me to maintain a spirit of gratitude, recognizing that every good and perfect gift flows from You. In times of challenge, remind me to focus on the blessings rather than the burdens, trusting in Your unwavering provision and care.

Grant me wisdom to cherish the gifts I have been given, the humility to share them freely with others, and the discernment to see how I can be effective. May my gratitude inspire generosity as I seek to reflect Your love and kindness in all that I do. Teach me to listen to the needs of those around me and respond with an open heart, becoming a channel of Your grace and compassion.

In seasons of struggle or scarcity, remind me of Your promises of provision. Let me find comfort in the knowledge that You are the source of all I need, sustaining me with Your boundless love and glory. Help me to resist fear and worry, staying rooted in the assurance that You walk with me through every trial.

May my gratitude not only live in my heart but be evident in my actions. Let it overflow into how I serve others, share my talents, and live a life that glorifies You. Guide me to use my gifts to uplift those around me, bringing hope, encouragement, and light wherever I go.

Thank You, Gracious Spirit, for the abundance of life and the immeasurable grace You pour into my days. May my gratitude be a constant prayer and may I always strive to share the blessings You have entrusted to me.

Please remain with me always.

Amen.

PURPOSE

Gracious Spirit,

I come before You with a heart open to Your guidance and a mind yearning for clarity. In the face of uncertainty, I seek the light of Your wisdom to navigate the challenges and choices before me.

My understanding is limited and I humbly ask for Your insight in all that I face. Illuminate my path so I may discern the choices that align with the greater purpose You have for my life. Grant me the patience to wait for Your answers, the courage to trust in Your timing, and the strength to act with faith when the moment comes.

As my soul needs guidance, cultivate within me a spirit of humility. Teach me to recognize and heed Your whispers in the quiet moments and through the people You place in my life. Surround me with wise counsel—those who reflect truth, love, and compassion—and help me learn from their experiences. Let each interaction deepen my understanding of Your purpose and the lessons You offer.

Grant me discernment in my relationships, my work, and the responsibilities I carry each day. Help me to look beyond immediate struggles and fleeting concerns to see the larger picture of Your presence at work in my life and the lives of others. May my choices be rooted in love, guided by wisdom, and filled with grace, so they reflect the light You shine in the world.

You remind me that You are a guide when there is no light. Let Your truth be a beacon, illuminating my way even when the road ahead feels uncertain or the journey feels long. Help me to trust in Your promises and take each step with confidence, knowing that I am never alone.

Thank You, Gracious Spirit, for hearing my prayer. I surrender my worries, fears, and anxieties to You, trusting in the comfort and clarity You bring. Walk with me as I move forward, helping me to find strength and hope in every step.

Please remain with me always.

Amen.

RENEWAL

Gracious Spirit,

In moments of darkness and despair, I turn to You, seeking the light of hope to guide me through. Life often feels overwhelming and I come to You now, longing for the comfort of Your presence and the assurance that I am not alone. Surround me with Your peace, reminding me that You are always near, even in my most trying times.

Help me look beyond my present difficulties and trust in the promise of renewal. You are the Spirit of new beginnings, the source of endless possibilities. Hope ignites within me, filling my heart with courage and resilience to face each day, just as the dawn rises faithfully each morning.

I lift those who are burdened by their circumstances, unable to see a way forward. For those who feel lost, hopeless, or broken, may they encounter the boundless grace and love that flows from You. Fill their hearts with calm, soothe their weary souls, and remind them of the healing power that is always within reach.

As I reflect on my own journey, help me to embrace the many seasons of life. Teach me to see beauty in the process of growth and transformation, even in the face of adversity. Let me find purpose in the challenges I endure, knowing that each step is part of a greater unfolding.

Grant me patience and faith, trusting that everything works together for good, in time. When doubts arise, anchor my hope firmly in You, the eternal source of strength and renewal.

Empower me to share this hope with others, becoming a beacon of encouragement and a reminder that no situation is beyond the reach of Your transformative grace.

Thank You for the renewal You bring to my spirit and the hope that sustains me. May I walk forward with faith, assured of Your presence and inspired by the promise of brighter days ahead.

Please do not leave me; remain with me as I navigate the path ahead.

Amen.

REPAIR

Gracious Spirit,

You are the essence of renewal, the source of strength and wholeness, and I open myself to Your transformative power to mend the brokenness within and around me.

I acknowledge the wounds I carry in my body, mind, and soul—wounds from past experiences, painful relationships, and my own choices. I ask for Your touch to bring me back to a place of balance and harmony. Help me release the grip of past hurts and offer forgiveness to those who have caused me pain, including myself. I know that forgiveness is the doorway to true healing, and I ask for the strength to step through it, releasing all bitterness and anger that weighs on my heart.

As I seek Your restoration, I recognize the fractures in my relationships. Teach me how to heal these connections with love, understanding, and humility. Guide me to communicate with compassion, to listen with an open heart, and to extend grace even when it is difficult. May Your energy flow through me, transforming me into an instrument of peace and reconciliation.

I lift all who are struggling—those who face physical illness, emotional pain, or spiritual distress. Surround them with Your comforting presence and infuse their hearts with hope. Let them find solace in moments of quiet assurance and strength in the promise of renewal. Use me too, as a channel of encouragement and kindness, offering support to those in need.

As I navigate my own journey of recovery, remind me of the beauty that remains in life. Open my eyes to the lessons pain can teach and the resilience that hardship can build. Let these challenges refine me so I emerge stronger, wiser, and ready to embrace the life You are guiding me toward.

Thank you for the promise of healing and the gift of restoration. I trust in the process, knowing each step brings me closer to the renewal I seek. Let my life become a living testament to the power of transformation and a reflection of the love that sustains me.

Please do not leave me; remain present as I continue forward, embracing this journey of change.

Amen.

RESILIENCE

Gracious Spirit,

Today I come seeking strength and resilience to face the obstacles that lie before me. I open myself to Your presence, asking for the power to rise when I am weary and to persevere when life feels overwhelming. Let Your energy fill the spaces where I feel weak and may Your presence steady me in moments of doubt.

Grant me the courage to confront my anxieties and the will to endure difficulties. Remind me that every challenge holds the potential for growth and that even my struggles can build the strength I need to move forward. Help me find purpose in my grief and wisdom in my trials so I may carry the lessons of today into a brighter tomorrow.

As I walk through life's challenges, remind me that I am never alone. Surround me with compassion, both from within and through the care of others who support me. Help me foster a spirit of resilience rooted in faith and hope, so I may rise again each time I stumble. Let Your light be my guide, shining even in the darkest of moments, reminding me of the path forward.

I lift all those who are struggling under the weight of their own burdens. May they find the strength to keep moving, even when the journey feels long and difficult. Bring hope to their hearts and remind them of the power of perseverance and faith. Help me to be a source of encouragement, offering support, kindness, and understanding to those in need.

Through every challenge, I choose to lean on the assurance of Your presence. I trust that there is a greater purpose unfolding, even in my hardest moments. Let my life reflect the resilience born from faith and the courage inspired by Your constant grace. May my journey inspire others to find their strength through hope and renewal.

Thank You for the promise that, with Your presence, I can endure all things. I trust in the unwavering support that surrounds me and I hold firmly to the light of transformation that You bring.

Do not leave me; remain near as I continue forward.

Amen.

RESTORATION

Gracious Spirit,

I surrender and breathe seeing the healing and restoration of my body, mind, and soul. You are the Great Spirit, the one who mends the broken and breathes life into the weary. In my pain and distress, I turn to You, trusting in Your ability to restore what is damaged and renew what feels depleted.

Touch me with Your healing hands. I lay before You all that burdens me — my spiritual struggles, emotional wounds, and physical ailments. You see the depths of my heart and understand my innermost needs. Help me release my troubles to You so that Your peace can flow over me like a gentle, cleansing stream.

Grant me patience and strength as I walk this path of healing; it reminds me that restoration is a journey, not an instant transformation. With each step, let me draw closer to You, finding opportunities to gain experience through the trials I face. Help me to see my pain as a testimony to Your faithfulness, turning my struggles into a witness of Your love and grace.

During this season, open my heart to the support of others. Surround me with compassionate souls who will encourage me and stand with me in my recovery. Let their kindness reflect Your love and may we uplift one another as we walk together in the light of Your Spirit.

As I heal, teach me to extend kindness and compassion to those around me. Let my journey be a source of hope and comfort to others, a reminder of the power of Your restoration. May

I be a vessel of Your love, offering solace and encouragement to those in need.

Thank You, Gracious Spirit, for Your unfailing mercy and the promise of renewal. You are my refuge and strength, and I trust in Your unwavering presence.

Please remain with me always.

Amen.

SATURATE

Gracious Spirit,

I turn to the boundless kindness and mercy that surrounds me. Before words are spoken, my needs, burdens, and heart are already known. I pray for a healing touch to restore my body, mind, and soul, renewing what has been broken and providing fresh strength.

Help me find serenity in this sacred presence and let love saturate every aching or worn part of me. As a comforting and compassionate Spirit, guide me in releasing suffering into divine hands.

Grateful for the hope, refuge, and healing offered, I trust in restoration, and rest in the promises made.

Please remain close, now, and always.

Amen.

SOURCE

Gracious Spirit,

You are my safeguard, my compass, and my strength. When the path ahead feels unclear, remind me that You have already prepared the way. Grant me courage and the wisdom to guide my thoughts, words, and actions in alignment with Your purpose.

Fill my heart with the peace that comes from trusting in You, even when life feels uncertain.

May Your love lift my spirit, giving me the grace and confidence to face each day with hope.

You are ever by my side: my unshakable foundation. Even when I cannot see, I trust in Your presence, knowing You are always with me.

Please stay close, now and forever.

Amen.

SURRENDER

Gracious Spirit,

None can compare to Your steadfastness. Ever-present and unchanging, You call to our hearts and guide us along paths of peace. In the face of challenges, temptations, and uncertainties, a way forward is revealed through Your grace. True freedom resides in Your presence and tranquility becomes the thread that binds us to all people and Creation.

Through every moment—past, present, and future—Your loving Spirit remains close. No matter where life leads or what has transpired, there is an enduring love that surpasses all earthly bonds, drawing our lives into one shared story.

Teach me to embrace life without fear, resting in the freedom that comes from trusting Your wisdom. Help me walk each day with quiet confidence, knowing divine love and guidance are ever near.

Please stay by my side, now and always.

Amen.

THANKSGIVING

Gracious Spirit,

I am walking today with a heart full of thanksgiving. I am deeply grateful for the blessings in my life, no matter how small. I cherish the beauty that surrounds me, the precious gift of life, and the love of family and friends.

Even in difficult moments, help me to recognize the abundance You have provided. Teach me to find joy in life's simple treasures — a warm sunrise, a kind word, or a moment of shared laughter. May I always remember that gratitude transforms my perspective and opens my heart to Your presence.

I pray for those who are struggling, pray that they, too, may find the strength to discover gratitude in their trials. Let my own expressions of thankfulness serve as a light, inspiring others to see the goodness in their own lives.

Thank You for Your unending kindness and love. I acknowledge that everything I have is a gift from You. In return, I commit to sharing these blessings with those around me, spreading Your love and light to a world in need.

Please stay by my side, guiding me in gratitude and grace.

Amen.

TRANQUILITY

Gracious Spirit,

I turn to You, Source of Peace, as life rages around me. In a world full of uncertainty, I long for the calm that only You can bring. Grant me the solace of knowing that You are my unwavering support and strength. Please calm my mind and heart. Remind me to seek You in moments of worry and anxiety, to rest in Your love and guidance. Encompass me in Your presence, soothing my soul and leading me to peace. Help me to trust in Your perfect timing and to release my burdens into Your capable hands.

Teach me to respond to conflict with empathy and understanding. Help me to cultivate a steady, calm mind that listens openly and approaches challenges with care. Even when peace feels difficult to hold onto, inspire me to be a source of light, striving to bring harmony wherever I go.

Guide me to be an advocate for unity in my relationships and a seeker of peace within myself. Let my compassion and love extend to all around me, creating an environment that nurtures kindness and care.

Shape my attitude to reflect Your grace so that my words and actions foster tranquility and understanding. May the peace I cultivate within radiate outward, transforming my surroundings into a sanctuary of calm.

Please do not leave me, O Spirit of Peace. Be my anchor and guide, now and always.

Amen.

TRUST

Gracious Spirit,

My new awareness has developed my faith and confidence in You. In a world of uncertainty and challenges, I seek Your direction to ground my spirit in the certainty of Your love and loyalty.

I recognize that there are times when uncertainty enters my heart and thoughts. I beg for Your assistance in overcoming these emotions and remembering that You are sovereign. Teach me to rely on You in times of fear and confusion, trusting that Your plans for me are excellent, even when I cannot see the big picture.

Help me create a faith-filled spirit that believes in the impossible and looks forward to what is ahead. I would like to remind You of the numerous ways You have worked in my life and the lives of others to strengthen my faith in Your goodness. Trust that the size of a mustard seed can move mountains, and that I remember this lesson as I deal with my own challenges.

Please direct my feet as I face life's uncertainty. Help me let go of my anxieties and find serenity in Your presence. I implore You to fill my heart with hope and confidence, allowing me to take courageous strides ahead, even when the way is uncertain.

As my faith grows, I hope to be able to encourage people around me. Let my faith in You encourage others to seek Your presence and feel Your love. May we walk in faith, supporting one another through life's challenges and accomplishments.

SHARON JONES, LMFT

Thank You for unchanging love and the gift of faith. I trust You because I know You are always there, guiding me. May my faith reflect Your glory and testify to Your magnificence.

Please do not leave me.

Amen.

WISDOM

Gracious Spirit,

I am open to knowledge and direction in my life. In moments of uncertainty, I turn to the fountain of all wisdom and insight, knowing my shortcomings and my deep need for divine guidance.

Grant me the discernment to align my choices and actions with Your will. Help me navigate life's complexities with purpose and grace. Remind me to seek Your counsel before I act, trusting in Your good and hopeful plans for me.

Empower me to hear the voice of truth above the clamor of the world around me. Teach me to recognize the gentle nudges of the Spirit that lead to fulfillment and growth. May I remain steadfast in the knowledge that You are always with me, even in times of doubt or fear.

Guide me to walk humbly, relinquishing my desire for control and trusting in Your perfect timing. I offer my goals and dreams to You, confident that You will direct my steps and lead me toward what is right. Even when the path ahead is unclear, I trust that all things work for my ultimate good.

Help me cultivate empathy and understanding for others as I pursue enlightenment. May the wisdom I gain from my divine encounters become a source of guidance and support for those around me. Let Your kindness and grace shine through my words and actions, inspiring others to listen for Your voice.

Teach me to be a peacemaker in my relationships and to seek harmony within myself. Let Your presence be my constant companion.

Please do not leave me.

Amen.

YOUR COMTEMPLATIVE SPACE

ACTION STEPS

ANSWERED PRAYER

BELIEFS

BLESSINGS

CARE

EVALUATE YOUR SPIRIT

HOPE

INTENTION

IGNITE THE FIRE

THOUGHTS

THANK YOU NOTES

MEET THE AUTHOR

Sharon Jones was born in Shreveport, Louisiana, and grew up in the small town of Coushatta. Her upbringing in this environment profoundly shaped her life and perspective. In search of a better life, Sharon decided to venture to San Francisco, taking a bus with only a handful of coins in her pocket. Sharon is a licensed marriage and family therapist based in California.

With over 30 years of experience in the behavioral health field, Sharon has worked in diverse settings, providing specialized therapies for the treatment of trauma, depression, and anxiety. Her therapeutic approach has offered comfort and hope to many people, creating a safe space for healing and personal growth.

Sharon's book, Alabaster Moments, celebrates those moments of transformation and healing in people's lives. Her writings have been included in several anthologies, such as House of Light, Divine Feminine Awakening, Wise Woman: International Day of the Girl Pandemic Edition, Powerful Women: Devotional Anthology of Powerful Prayers, and Rising Above Narcissistic Abuse. Through her work and words, Sharon continues to inspire and guide those seeking meaningful change in their lives.

Made in the USA
Columbia, SC
11 February 2025